Of the Festivity

Volume 55 of the
Yale Series of Younger Poets.
Edited by W. H. Auden
and published on the
Mary Cady Tew Memorial Fund

William Dickey

Of the
Festivity

Foreword by W. H. Auden

New Haven: Yale University Press, 1959

Library of Congress catalog card number: 59–6795.

ACKNOWLEDGMENTS: For permission to reprint
certain of these poems, my thanks are due to
"Poetry: A Magazine of Verse," "The Hudson Review,"
"New Mexico Quarterly," "Western Review," and
"Prairie Schooner." I have also to thank the Corporation of Yaddo
for affording me an opportunity to complete the book.

This book is for my father.

Foreword

Since this is the last year in which I shall be editing the Yale Series of Younger Poets, I hope Mr. Dickey will forgive me for taking this foreword to his book as an opportunity to make a few valedictory observations.

Who should edit a series of this kind? The answer is easy. He should be someone with such a passionate desire to discover new talent that he spends his days reading every Little Magazine, every pamphlet published by tiny presses which he can lay his hands on; he should be gifted with an infallible nose for detecting the difference between the genuine and the spurious novelty; *and* he should be without the slightest desire to write a line of poetry himself.

A practicing poet is never a perfect editor: if he is young, he will be intolerant of any kinds of poetry other than the kind he is trying to write himself; if he is middle aged, the greater tolerance of his judgment is offset by the decline of his interest in contemporary poetry. The books which interest him most are unlikely to be books of poetry, and when he does read poems for pleasure, they are likely to be of a date and style as far removed from the contemporary as possible. As an editor, therefore, however conscientious he may try to be in appraising the manuscripts submitted to him, he will not and cannot, as an ideal editor should, go on the hunt for more and better manuscripts because he does not know where to look. Since, alas, the ideal editor does not exist, a practicing poet over the age of thirty-five is perhaps the best second-best, but he should be changed fairly frequently.

Whatever his virtues or defects, any editor of the Yale Series of Younger Poets will face problems which are not of his making and which he is powerless to solve.

He can only select the best manuscript from those submitted to him, yet he knows that there are probably a number of poets around without a published book whose work may well be better.

Perhaps they have never heard of the Yale Press or perhaps, having seen some of its previous publications, they have no wish to be seen in such company.

Then, he can only choose one manuscript a year to publish. This can be most unfair. During my period as editor, there have been years when there were several volumes I should have been glad to publish, and there was one year when not a single one seemed good enough.

Few people, on retiring from a position, can resist offering advice to their successors, who probably do not want it and will not heed it. Accordingly, I shall pass on to mine, for his imaginary benefit, a description of my procedure upon receiving in the spring a heavy parcel of manuscripts by names unknown to me.

First Reading

The first time I go through them, I try to exclude from my mind any such considerations as originality, style, taste, or even sense, while I look for one thing only, *lines* of poetry. By this I mean a line which speaks itself, which, as it were, no longer needs its author's help to exist.

Thus, in my first reading of Mr. Dickey, I came upon lines like

> *Spinning and smiling as the world diminished*
>
>   .   .   .   .   .
>
> *That showed him whole, when we had gone away*
>
>   .   .   .   .   .
>
> *Their husbands carve the dressing and the bird,*
> *The day, the napkin, and the carving plate*
> *To bits that are too little to be heard.*

whereupon he went onto the pile of potential winners. It is possible to show evidence of great intelligence and sensibility but to be lacking in the first power essential to poetry, the power to *speak*. Mr. Dickey's lines have both.

Second Reading

By now the number of manuscripts is considerably reduced. Again I read through them, looking for only one thing, the power to notice, the possession of what one might call uncommon common sense. This may appear either as an accurate and vivid description of some creature or object which we have all seen or as a truthful and illuminating comment upon some experience with which we are all familiar. For example, everyone carries some scar or other upon his body, but it is Mr. Dickey and not everyone who makes this observation:

> *Like hasty marks on an explorer's chart:*
> *This white stream bed, this blue lake on my knee*
> *Are an angry doctor at midnight, or a girl*
> *Looking at the blood and trying not to see*
> *What we both have seen. Most of my body lives,*
> *But the scars are dead like the grooving of a frown,*
> *Cannot be changed, and ceaselessly record*
> *How much of me is already written down.*

The capacity to notice is not, like the power to speak, essential to all poetry—there are beautiful lyrics in which it plays no part at all—but I value it very highly in this age as a *moral* virtue.

Almost every aspect of modern life tends to alienate us, poets and nonpoets alike, from a common world and shut us up with our subjective selves, a tendency which is aggravated, not cured, by the writer who likes to think of himself as *engagé*. The only proper resistance is the cultivation of a dispassionate passion to see things as they are and to remember what really happened. We all need each other's help in this matter and whenever a poet makes me recognize something in our common world which I could have recognized for myself but did not, I am grateful.

Third Reading

Having satisfied myself that the author of a manuscript can make words speak and is interested in something more than his precious little self, I now read it poem by poem, looking to see if he has learned to write a whole poem and has written enough of them to be ready to publish a book. How many is enough? Remembering that, when reading a volume by the greatest and most famous names, one almost always says of some of the poems "Why did he include that?" but that one never says this about a volume of one's own, I regard a manuscript as meriting publication if I like a third of its contents.

Like any work of art, a successful poem is a complete world with which, though it is a thing, the reader can make personal contact. But poetry is peculiar in that it is made of words; the medium of this art is the same as that of guidebooks, treatises on plumbing, business correspondence, and the *Congressional Record*. A poem therefore is, necessarily, what a painting need not be and a piece of music cannot be, a double world of things (words) and meanings. "Pure" poetry, poetry, that is to say, in which word and meaning are identical, is an impossibility; even a lyric like "Full Fathom Five" is "representational." Further, since the meaning of words depends upon common social agreement, poetry is the most "traditional" of all the arts. No poet can invent a language of his own; even the puns in *Finnegans Wake* presuppose an unchanging traditional language. Assuming that he had learned to speak French, the shade of Homer would have little difficulty, I believe, in reading the poetry of Rimbaud; he might not like it but he would know why. But a Greek musician confronted with a piece by Webern, let us say, would be unable to pass any judgment whatsoever, because he would hear no musical sounds, only noises.

Thus while in the other arts an original vision may often seem to be the result of a change of style or method, in poetry an original and in itself nonverbal vision seems the necessary precondition for a change in the handling of the language.

Most arguments about *how* poetry should be written seem to me futile because they conceal the real difference between the parties, which is their respective notions of the proper poetical subject, what poetry should be *about*.

As an example of one of Mr. Dickey's poems, let me cite "Part Song, with Concert of Recorders." I choose it because it is a song, and of all kinds of poetry songs are the least personal and most verbal.

This poem is a little ballad, a melodramatic dialogue between a lady and her doctor-lover, who has just murdered her husband. In each of the seven five-line stanzas, the first line ends with the word *there* or *where,* the fourth and fifth lines with the word *care.*

> *She*   *And he lies dead—*
> *He*   *His blood is seeping there—*
> *She*   *Where we have kissed—*
> *He*   *Where we have done much more—*
> *She*   *I liked it best the way it was before.*
> *He*   *You like it now.*
> *She*   *I like it, but I care.*
> *He*   *No longer care.*
>
>   . . . . .
>
> *She*   *Come, Doctor, we must fly someotherwhere.*
> *He*   *I have my bag full of essential things,*
>   *False passports, currency, and diamond rings—*
> *She*   *True pledge of love for those who truly care.*
> *He*   *Who live and care.*

A lucky chance of the English language gave Mr. Dickey two rhyme words which can be used in a number of different senses, but his use of them, and of a simple, melodramatic situation which might all too easily have been ridiculous, to compose a poignant and resonant parable comes from his personal vision, not the English language.

At present, to judge from this volume, Mr. Dickey's speciality is nightmare worlds described in the simplest possible diction.

> *Both of these women are fat. Anchovy paste*
> *Is the staple of their helter-skelter meals,*
> *And other things rich or alien to the taste,*
> *Cheap salmon roe, cream, the meat of eels.*

Moon-disks, they smile at each other over the dishes
Vast buttery smiles of appetite and love;
In a hazy light they swim like cannibal fishes,
Each waits for each to make the precipitate move.

This satisfies the three demands I have made in my readings: the lines speak, something has been noticed, and speech and observation have become the servants of a personal vision.

In conclusion, one more teaser for my editorial successor. Suppose that one year he is confronted with two manuscripts which seem to him of equal merit. He can publish only one. How, then, is he to make his choice? The only criterion in such a case, so far as I can see, is the variety of the Series. I would choose whichever of the two was, stylistically, the least like the winning manuscripts of the previous three years. But could one dare tell the author of the rejected manuscript this? No, let him attribute his rejection to the editor's bad taste.

W. H. AUDEN

Contents

Part One

The Dolls Play at Hansel and Gretel

I

They hunch their heads against the fable of night,
Their thin wax heads with eyes that are too large;
Each one examines the bruises of the day.

When they are through with this they take their parts;
This one is witch and this one is the wood,
Trees flit into his huddled brain, and owls.

And the poor children, the senseless, shabby things,
Cluttered with pebbles that will do no good,
Lift their rag hands and imitate despair:

"Why have you put us out into the cold?
All day, helpless as any human child,
We have been yours to fondle or destroy.

You made us saints or thieves or prostitutes,
You put us slyly in Jocasta's bed;
Mother and father, what we are is yours.

We fought the wars you could not fight alone,
But at the end of the garden you said go,
And we sprawled nameless in the pitying flowers.

Now in the dark the *Doppelgänger* winks
To say the path goes on as it always has.
Bushes take foot, and the wood closes in."

11. The Witch's Song

In the epileptic fit
When your bones were scarcely knit
You beheld the paradise
Of my parti-colored eyes.

In the foul delirium
When the cockatrices come,
Eager to delay the truth
You have kissed my withered mouth.

Now let hand release its hold
On the world you have been told,
Let the sleeping eyelid fall
Shutting out the sight of all.

Coiling in the middle ear,
Let my word be what you hear,
Let my hand that sews and clips
Snip your tongue and stitch your lips.

In my body you will find
Mathematics of the blind,
Malformations there and scars
Of the potent integers.

In the crevice of my gown
Secret lies your mortal town,
In the science of my breast
Is your formula of rest.

III. The Gingerbread House's Song

Wind the thread and wind the thread,
Mother married with a sailor,
And I thought that I was dead
If her common sense could fail her.
But I buttoned up my fright
And I strangled him at night.

Turn the spool and turn the spool,
Father took a witch for daughter.
Then I knew he was a fool—
Witches can't cross running water.
Like an angel in a dream
I immersed her in the stream.

Sing the song and sing the song,
All the nightingales are hidden.
Right is right and wrong is wrong,
Folk must do what they are bidden
Or I take them by the neck
And I put them in my sack.

Cast the stone and cast the stone,
Eat the muscle and the marrow,
Eat the body to the bone,
It will rise again tomorrow
Worshiping the hand that slew,
And had every right to do.

Close the eye and close the eye,
All things come to him that wishes.
Now the world is only I
I am finding it delicious.
Powerful, virile, handsome, young,
I taste the blood upon my tongue.

iv. The Oven's Song

The toad
Glitters in the night
From the jewel in its head.
Everything else is dead.
I did not bring you.
I will not take you.
Fancies of lunacy glitter in your head.

Only the same door
From the same room and into the same room.
Under this time
It is the same time that it was before
When you came and will come.
Circle the stone with marks to mark your time.
You will remember nothing of them here.

Only the box,
And the locks,
And the nail.
You are unwounded yet, but you will fail.
As soon as you start to know, the wounds will come,
Blood in the pricked thumb,
Blood on the shirt,
Till all of you is drained and put aside,
Folded like paper on a shelf.

You are yourself.
Cuddle into my entrail and be still.
There is no tie between you and my will,
But an indifference.
What you hear
Runs on as steady in my ear
As the noise made by an indifferent machine.
I will not say what you have been,

That is concern, and I am not concerned.
I am the toad's jewel in the center of the skull.
I am what you have earned.

v

Their thin wax heads are scattered on the grass,
Their button eyes look dully at the sky
Where it has begun to rain. The morning comes.

Empty and destitute, they disarrange
The order of life, until the children come
Telling them what are their identities.

For Easter Island or Another Island

We are the last that there are anywhere.
The changeless figures, the great heads sitting on stones,
Look out of place. We, too, who put them there
Look out of place, ribbed in these cages of bones
Where the heart hangs and hangs like a yellow gourd,
And the eyes, divest of covering, lean and sway;
Throat's edge shines out bright as the edge of a sword.
We are the last. Everyone goes away.

They fall like leaves, the cities of the past,
Endlessly into rock and the endless streams.
Our minds fall shut on each, fall at the last
With the great-lipped faces of our merciless dreams
In the red-colored dust. It with its various reds
Like the first leap of anger fills our heads.

For My Grandfather, Dead

Then let him go.
Wherever he would go, gone, somewhere other,
Out, in a child's green world, in a lamb's morning
He rose. Almost still dark. But in his way
In the faint smother of high-risen great clouds dawning
On the jubilant acres, in the cries of the day's
First finery with cows hushed in the sleeping stables
Like a tall love for everything of it he goes
Servant of beasts in a warm morning glory
Welcome of sun.

Then let him go.
Into the hill's grave in the high air clearly
Reflecting from water, washing with figures of light.
Around him his hands leave his patterns, his scything, and nearly
Now he is one of them, lain with his sweet mute
Birds and kind beasts in the most loving fable,
Here in queer tangle of flower and fresh root
Sipping the earth, sleeping deeply, asleep to recall
How in the night's last hour they would murmur and stir
For the sight of the child's sun hurrying to them all.

The Self Prepares for an Unwilling Journey

The Dioscuri guard you in this passing;
Being half of heaven and half of hell they know
What hurries you to your shamefaced undressing,
Why your respectable fingers rattle so.

Though night, touched by a bulb that grimes the ceiling,
Is in you and around you where you stand,
You cannot hope for any new concealing;
This hand that reaches for you is your hand,

This body yours that has been twin in anger
And that walked out of you and lived apart
Doing violence to the accepted stranger;
Leaving you peaceful in your arbored heart,

Spinning and smiling as the world diminished,
As the great rages beckoned, but swept past.
The dog howls at the doorstop. This is finished.
Now you are in the room of the very last

And have the perfect partner for your dances,
Knowing the steps that no one else has known,
The opened minutes and regretted chances,
Knowing you to the engraving of your bone.

The Dioscuri guide you to your bedding.
Twice-fixed in heaven and hell, they see, and send
Impossible starlight to describe your wedding,
And the long fire to reconcile your friend.

G.F. Died 1954, Aged 27

> . . . *e parve di costoro*
> *quegli che vince e non colui che perde.*

Now deeply drunk, always where you have found him
In any place before, he will lie dead,
Thin hair spilt in a yellow pool around him
Beneath the night light, his arms under his head:
His face jerks with the quickening dream that holds him.

He looked for people to kiss. Someone uncertain called him
To a hidden door less innocent than his eyes.
The lingering smile of that red-lit night appalled him,
But whirled him, after his nausea of surprise,
Into the pattern of the dream that holds him.

Now he moves downward. Hundreds of mouths beside him
Spit truths at his too-knowledgeable face;
Hearing the hot birds and the voices of beasts deride him
He weaves helplessly, cries, stumbles out of this place
Over the threshold, into the dream that holds him.

He dies in the body. The various bones that made him
Loose gradually from their connected forms.
The shape of flesh that mimicked him and hid him
Ruins past the touch of sensual alarms,
Commends him, finally, into the dream that holds him.

Maybe all are angels there, and soar together
On steep wings, day after day speaking of love,
Or in the hushed nights of deep, motionless weather
Lie by each other gently kissing, and move
Like white stars into the dark of the dream that holds them.

Where will you go now, anywhere, not to find him?
He is drunk so deeply that he does not stir.
As the day goes, he goes, and leaves behind him
All things but sleep, to start that passage for
The summer country of the dream that holds him.

Quae lucis miseris tam dira cupido? Dicam.

But high above, the word "Love" cried
By angels in precipitous places;
I am the part of me that died
Putting the racehorse through his paces,
Driving the car across the tracks,
Lying out blue in the best-room bed.
I am that unhappy part that lacks
All the gentility of the dead
And cannot see, and cannot see
Where the love is to comfort me.

And demons in the depth cry "Love"
Mournfully, with distorted faces;
Sea elephants and beasts that move
With clumsy dignity seek their places,
Choired in their impulse to adore
The fact of rot and dissolution.
I am the thing I was before,
Fixed in my fleshly constitution,
And cannot hear, and cannot hear
The word that echoes at my ear.

The gods and goddesses, rank on rank,
Range in their several states and graces;
I am the flesh that dying stank,
Stinking, was thrown to charnel places.
This meat the mumbling lip of worm
Draws back from, having wholly fed;
The frail bones leave their cage of form,
Finding the new shape of the dead.
Only the small, unmoving mind
Cries for me, being left behind.

And stars look out like ordered eyes
Into their claim, their different spaces,
Exulting as each body dies,
Glad for the wind from emptied places,
Where what was good has yet gone by,
Though beautiful, yet did not stay,
But fell, as through a rim of sky
Into the blind, continuous day,
And cannot know, and cannot know
What is was like to have been so.

Love hammers totally at the ear
From snails' horns, from seraphic faces,
From every beast of sea and air,
From pinions, fins, from carapaces,
All caught in that unthinking sound,
All moving with that simple motion
In positive certainty around
Axes of positive devotion,
And I must be, and I must be,
Now of this only company.

Forget the voice with which I sing
But sing, forget the dancing paces
But dance, forget there was a spring
Before this summer's large embraces.
You innocence of hand and eye,
Pleasures of satin or of sight,
Now go, letting me put you by
For the severeness of this light
Where I may praise, where I may praise
Love in the clean, unending days.

Part Two

Part Song, with Concert of Recorders

I

SHE   Doctor, I did not see that you were there.
HE   Madam, I've stabbed your husband in his bed.
        He now makes one with the unhouseled dead.
        I come to have you tell me that you care.
SHE   You know I care.

II

SHE   I did not know you when you came in there.
HE   I did not then intend that you should know,
        Thought in the dark I'd have my way and go,
        But love has come upon me and I care.
SHE   Tell me you care.

III

SHE   Who made you come and find the door to there?
        Who made you turn that handle and come in?
        What we have done, what we do, it is sin;
        We shall be punished for it; have a care.
HE   I cannot care.

IV

SHE   And I, who lay so warm and quiet there—
HE   And you, who grew excited with my kiss—
SHE   Who would have thought that it would come to this?
        Let all be circumspect before they care.
HE   But let them care.

V

SHE And he lies dead—
HE   His blood is seeping there—
SHE Where we have kissed—
HE   Where we have done much more—
SHE I liked it best the way it was before.
HE   You like it now.
SHE   I like it, but I care.
HE   No longer care.

VI

BOTH For we have gone a curious way from there,
      But we have love and so we go ahead.
      It does no good to think about the dead.
      What's dead is dead, it will not ever care
      As we can care.

VII

SHE Come, Doctor, we must fly someotherwhere.
HE   I have my bag full of essential things,
     False passports, currency, and diamond rings—
SHE True pledge of love for those who truly care.
HE   Who live and care.

Les très riches heures

The duke rides in a green, enameled wood;
Jewels called birds elaborate his trees,
All colors meet to do him courtesies,
And intricate shadows pattern to his mood.
Is it the world we would all have if we could?
Innocent of doubt, of angularities;
Perspective here is a diligence to please
So pure it cannot be misunderstood.

Somewhere behind that picture is the court,
The palace stinking like a royal sty.
But it was the subliming counterpart
That led its dance across the painter's eye,
Whose silver boar seems to admire the sport
And the perilous, delicate huntsmen riding by.

Footnote to Caesar's Wars

Hercynian elk have rigid knees
As straight as the Hercynian trees;
They cannot bend them as they please.

So when they sleep, as sleep they must
(Sleep comes to all among the just;
Elk are God's children too, I trust),

They seek a patch of woodland sunk
In peace, and having dined and drunk
They lean on a convenient trunk.

(What dreams about the elk may hover
Of worthy foe or bashful lover,
Authority does not discover.)

But when the elk at spring of day
Enormously have strode away
To elkly duties, or to play,

Hercynian hunters, small and wizen,
Who monstrously themselves bedizen
With animal skulls, have also risen,

Have tracked the elk (elk tracks are plain),
Have cut their trees almost in twain
Till only *imagos* remain.

The elk return, show no surprise
At trees which wear their natural guise,
Lean, fall, and cannot then arise.

Some flee; some, on the other hand,
Gathered in a pathetic band,
Beseech the fallen elk to stand.

Although themselves in mortal fear
Of toppling should they get too near,
They stay a hopeless minute here,

Then drift into the woody haze,
There to become extinct, and graze
No more as in J. Caesar's days,

Leaving the world more commonplace
Without the tragicomic grace
Of love in an ungainly race.

The Lady of Shalott, Her Mirror Broken

Species of common garden cat, who are
You moaning for among the vegetables?
Your ears lie geometrically flat,

Flat as the tops of innumerable strait tables;
And your mouth bursts with its interminable cry
In the growing voices that the garden babbles

Of vine and weed and bean you break. And why?
There is no love lies hidden in its heart,
But the squat stone god Terminus is smiling by,

Telling you of ends and boundaries and part
Of the ways you cannot get out and no one in.
Will you stop it now? There was no reason to start.

There's no outside, no others, nothing in
All your life left empty; strut and stride
Here in the carrots where you can be clean

Like the proper guardian of a proper pride.

Obstinacy of Water

The glass-like water like a pier-glass swayed
When we were gone, and angry rocks stopped breaking
The unison of reflecting, and a quilted,
Proud aboriginal swan pranced from his place of hiding
To bobble on great peaks and flowers of water
That showed him whole, when we had gone away.

The Plot

Beatrice lay naked on the narrow bed;
"I'm half in love with easeful death," she said.
"And so am I," I said without delay,
"But once you've got him, how will you make him stay?"
"By woman's wiles, and by ambitious kisses;
He can't be satisfied with those skeleton blisses,
Those beds on which an atomy reposes—
I'll give him flesh like concentrate of roses.
The change will make a man of him again."
"I grant you that," I said. "What happens then?"
"Then I deceive him carefully," she said;
"I leave him soundly sleeping, and I tread
On airy foot in search of certain potions,
Somniferous drugs and faint Lethean lotions.
I scatter poppy near him as he slumbers,
I tell off charms and cabalistic numbers—"
"He sleeps?" "He sleeps forever and a day,
He sleeps the ages of the world away."
"He leaves us free for our desired pursuing?"
"He leaves us free for doing and undoing;
And safe from traveling through that ominous portal,
We'll have our pleasure, mortal and immortal."

Which Door? Which Door?

Here every bottle cries O drink me quickly,
The leaves are shaped like arrow points, the eye
Befurred with drugs looks around only thickly,
The Rabbit mutters it is time to die.

Innocent Alice in this queasy mirror
Displays the breastworks of a Minoan jade;
Everything one can hear will mock the hearer,
Everything one can make will be unmade.

The Rabbit mutters and the night arises;
It must have been the wrong hole after all.
Certainly this one holds no nice surprises,
Only the consequences of the fall.

Questions about a Spaniel of Eleven

After the operation she grew hair
At a terrible rate; her hormone balance changed.
She barked more in the night, became estranged
From children; if she found them prying there
Under the kitchen table where she slept
She snarled, trying to snap them out of sight.
She was convinced that only she was right.
At times her eyes ran, and we said she wept.

Seeing the old maid in the dog is odd.
The great ears stay the same, the anxious poise
Pattering up at mealtime. But the voice
Has changed and whines. Is she convinced of God
And the righteous sterility of her aging tongue?
Or would she rather have married, and died young?

Exploration over the Rim

Beyond that sandbar is the river's turning.
There a new country opens up to sight,
Safe from the fond researches of our learning.
Here it is day; there it is always night.

Around this corner is a certain danger.
The streets are streets of hell from here on in.
The Anthropophagi and beings stranger
Roast in the fire and meditate on sin.

After this kiss will I know who I'm kissing?
Will I have reached the point of no return?
What happened to those others who are missing?
Oh, well, to hell with it. If we burn, we burn.

Part Three

Of the Festivity

Outside, a verandah gives upon a court
Full of tin cans and whistles. Over hill
The noise of nubile screaming shreds the night.
Not any thing about this place is still;
The presentation of the virgins sounds
Harsh as a sacrifice, heavy with blood
In the stone stables of boys where they gleefully fall.

Can we come out of that sober at all?
That ape distortion with its talking wounds,
That putting off the human for the dog?
Out in the street the frightened sirens call;
Crowds gather. The high diver dives for good,
Bloody in his incendiary fall.

Here there are only the two of us, and we—
Do we know any better than they why we have met?
And your hand lifting the glass, leaving a wet
Stain on the broken table, is it there
In anything beside a minute's heat,
Some sight that in the mirror edge will change?
I walk through silver, knowing it is strange,
Hoping you are on my side of the glass
And I can touch you and you not be less.

Afraid of words, the tenderness of words
That come to the lips out of their own accord—
Here peace must marry with the violent sword,
Its violence collected to repose,
And all the words my mouth has ever said
Will fail to tell us whether we live or die;
But that mouth close on your throat is comforted
And in your softness finds no perjury.

31

In time of war, the men of virtue go
Apart to fight the war of their good will,
And in the Saturnalia there is still
The center moment, full of silences,
The eye, the constancy, the generous part,
The gift moving equally within the heart.

Mere touch is truth, when it can echo so,
In lightning bridge the compass of our sky;
Your hand light on my shoulder is the flow
Of everything you have done, and learned thereby,
Your mouth the echo of your childhood mouth.
Kissing with all the years that are between
We taste the intricate pattern of our growth,
The cruel or devious persons we have been,
And are accepted in our shamefastness,
Not being more than human, and not less.

Naked between the angel and the beast,
Explore the limits of our continent—
Under the arching of the bodiless air
Here is the undivided element,
Earlier than day and night can cleave apart,
Older than we, but given to us now
For us in the slight body to make new
With sound and touch, with the arrest that came
In the recognition of our single name.

Put out the light. Somewhere the morning stirs.
Outside the world is dead or gone to sleep.
Still on their branches stand the sleeping birds;
On the verandah the still air lies steep.
And in the room, the murmur is of sleep.
Lie close, lie quiet, weary and undistressed,
Kissing the hand that hollows to your breast.

Silver Creek Falls

Watching the stream come spilling over its ledge,
The very point where it falls, your eyesight changes.
Only in idea is there such an edge,
A dividing line, because the water lunges
Past it all of the time and is not the same.
Form is the slave of motion, not its king,
And what we name as if it had an object's name
Is only an accident of that journeying.

Turn, having looked too long, and you cannot find
Even shadows of the world you called your own;
Interior shadows marry in your mind
With the swift circumstance of changing stone,
And your dimension is to recognize
Elements in their own continual air:
Outside the apparatus of your eyes
The water that only by vanishing is there.

Memoranda

The scars take us back to places we have been,
Cities named Masochism or Inaccuracy.
This little one between the finger and the thumb
Is something that my brother did to me
On a hot Washington's Birthday in the past,
When we were young and cruelly competent;
In a miniature world like a glass fishing float
He was the total image of intent.

Who stuck the pencil point into my palm?
It is so long ago that I cannot say,
But the black stick of graphite under the skin—
Some friend, some enemy put it there that way
To succeed in calling himself always to mind.
Action has consequence, and though his face
Has faded into the city of the lost,
I look at my hand and see the injured place.

Like hasty marks on an explorer's chart:
This white stream bed, this blue lake on my knee
Are an angry doctor at midnight, or a girl
Looking at the blood and trying not to see
What we both have seen. Most of my body lives,
But the scars are dead like the grooving of a frown,
Cannot be changed, and ceaselessly record
How much of me is already written down.

Étude: Andantino

Beyond the railroad trestle is the river.
That is the middle voice. The one still farther
Is in the town, shining out toward the water.
The middle voice we hear. The other voices,
As of impatient lovers who still wander,
Are muted by our being here together.

In dark we come, to watch slow-moving water,
Partly imprisoned by the indolent river,
Partly still free interminably to wander.
We might go with it, or go even farther
By its side moving swiftly and together,
Supposing we were called by far-off voices—

No, not this night. This is no night to wander.
Lie still and watch the circles in the water
Dislimn and form again; all now together
Tickling the whole long body of the river.
It is as if it could speak with a hundred voices,
Close by at first, but slowly getting farther.

The nights when you and I have been together
Watching the flashes where the fireflies wander,
Quiet as if we had no need for voices,
Are like a dream of slowly circling water,
Always at rest yet always moving farther,
Are like the compass of an endless river.

The voices that you hear are not our voices
But one that is the voice of us together,
Meaning more than we are and reaching farther.
The words from lip to lip equally wander,
Moving from source to stream, to a quick river,
And fade, and are the murmur of the water.

I see you dimly, yet I see you farther
Than in the day's loud eyes and hungry voices,
Than in the hot spate of that human river
Where we can be but cannot be together,
As here we are, hearing the voice of water,
Deep in the twilight where all lovers wander.

Safe and together, toward intrusive voices
Like troubled water, may we never wander;
But let the river bear us gently farther.

Twenty Years Gone,
She Returns to the Nunnery

The color bleaches from her hair;
Once black, she is now wholly fair.
Housewives who cried her out a whore
Find her not as she was before.

And changed the color of her breast;
Feeling too naked, she has dressed
Herself up over the collarbone
Into a reticence of gown.

Now in her face the smile is white
Like pure transparencies of light,
And disappear the copious red
Kisses she gave in her dark bed.

All is renewed about her form
Since mortal body took no harm,
Moved by an aptitude too clear
For argument to reach her ear.

Finally she comes where she would come,
Enters this house she went out from,
And in the cavern of her breast
Her heart lies like a lamb at rest.

The tall men fade, the dark men dare
No longer to inhabit her,
Who is now made the tenement
Of a more masculine intent.

Lesson of the Master

As much as he could learn has done no good.
Where the complexities started, there he stands,
Looking attentively at his two hands
That ought to point the way out of the wood.
They point to nothing. They curl in and rest.

Around him in the thicket bird and beast
Give birth or die in a repeated way;
God moulds the human animal out of clay.
The animal takes breath, then does its best.
Its best is good enough. Its bones decay.

The animal put by, how will he know—
Lacking that murderous heart—the innocent track?
Who knows enough to walk forward or walk back?
Generations of chattering mannikins sprout and grow
While he stands reasoning the first attack.

As much as he could learn has done no good.
Logic of Aristotle fills his brain;
Non-Aristotelian monkey noises reign
Carnal and bloody in that primitive wood
Where his hands twitch and then curl in again.

One Incident of Many

Turning clumsily into the embrace
She finds herself stopped by uncertainty.
It is not so dark that she cannot see his face
Looking up into the rain. Can he suppose that she
Came toward this kiss without encouragement?
Has she been reading into his every act
What she wants, and only cold kindliness was meant?

The night is like a tunnel around her head.
She is in love, it is the time for her
To be reassured. He is like something dead.
Surely if she speaks that nothingness will stir,
Take her in its arms, be man, sweat and desire,
Show her the mutual fire to her fire.

She is quiet. It was wrong to want what anyone gets.
No, he will say, somehow you've misunderstood.
If she beats her hands against him he will be good,
Saying, it was my fault, saying, one forgets
How it is. She has forgotten herself again,
Thinking something important had supplanted her.
She is as ignorant as ever, and as plain.

The night will pass, with its possibility;
The trees that seemed for a moment neutral there
In the fresh burst of the stayed, certain air
Will lash and cringe about her face as she
Turns up the path she has turned up before,
Hurries, holding her coat about her head.
He need not trouble to see her to her door.

Part Four

Minotaur

Gone from the unbelievable noise, where girls
Lash pallid hair moodily to and fro,
Gone to the creeper where the night owls go,
Where the busy bee-stung lip in anger curls.

I am the overhanger, he who whirls
You giddy in the summer afterglow,
That round eye gleaming on the winter snow,
That cracked laugh rising in the tidal swirls:

Where you will meet me first is no great matter,
A casual leaf that flutters in your face,
A spider or a dog. More like the latter,
Running, and all at once it is a race,
And where you turn, I win, and in that place
I shall learn silence, and you will learn grace.

A Vision, Caged

Over the city beneficent drugs conspire
To give the murderous one more night at large.
Their absolute senses tremble at the verge,
See the just crime, the unavoidable fire
Burning the mother of two. From ward to ward
The blanket of sedation settles in
Like generous, strangling hands. Pick any card—
Once again now the action will begin.
Punch will love Judy till he breaks her skull,
Mother hit Father with the parlor chair;
Their cup of interest completely full,
All of the watching children will be there.
Night falls. The exhibitionist displays
To his tight brain the gestures that release;
Grey in the midst of institutional greys
The alcoholic lurches into peace.
Nurses like ships' sails borne on the full breeze
Loom momentarily up and disappear.
Where disappears. All of these minds, at ease,
Congratulatory, concentrate on here,
The moment of the crime, the moment when
Suddenly a buried life broke out to flower.
The bloody children are a might-have-been
Compared to the importance of that hour,
Compared to the feeling that at least it's done—
Thank God the impetus to it can run down
And say, "Dear child, good-night," and then the one
Need is to find a corner of your own—
The corner grows enormous in their sight,
The lovely hypodermic brims and spills
Straight to the heart. Heart's engines fill the night,
Ever and again it swells, it hates, it kills.

Amazons

Both of these women are fat. Anchovy paste
Is the staple of their helter-skelter meals,
And other things rich or alien to the taste,
Cheap salmon roe, cream, the meat of eels.

Moon-disks, they smile at each other over the dishes
Vast buttery smiles of appetite and love;
In a hazy light they swim like cannibal fishes,
Each waits for each to make the precipitate move.

Music will cloy them if it is played too loudly;
They want to hear only an intimate hum
As it were, in the gut, that consummate and deadly,
Gives them good earnest of the food to come.

Canonical Hours

The ladies of the morning gauze their mouths
With little filmy napkins and are still.
Their husbands live in shells of simple truths,
Perennial explosions of the will.

And through the morns the ample ladies gather
The ribbons of their lives and press them clear.
They are intrinsic selves and need no other
Posture to arrive and interfere.

So through the layers of the afternoons
They warm themselves like giant oven cakes,
And at the patter of enamel spoons
Each stirs and momentarily awakes,

Joining herself in union with her kind,
Feeling the comfortable corset of their thought;
She moves like pilot fish among her mind
Seeking the aboriginal cachalot.

The ladies sit at evening satiate.
Their husbands carve the dressing and the bird,
The day, the napkin, and the carving plate
To bits that are too little to be heard.

Cassandra

This is because I am spiteful. You see, I hate
What hates me: houses, women with children, serpents, stones
Ringed viciously round with their blemishes looking me over:
What they do is too late now, nothing atones,
Nothing helps when the high god hate hits out at the sides
    of my head
And in moans with my tongue like a tripped snare dangling
    before
I sum them chapter and verse of their intricate ends.

But nothing ends. All of their war-splintered bones
I cry like candies or kisses the length of their towns,
All of the blood on the street spilt still will not let itself fall
Where I see it will be: it is all
Ahead, hard, terrible, simple to see but to tell?

Yet I will tell what I see:
Craft coiling like night in a pit, like a murderous bird's skull's
Word for their ear: will they hear? will the sweet smile
Stop on their lips where their grave-teeth now are beginning
    to grow?
Once they are dead I am free. I shall know

What I know now in a harmless historian's mouth,
Saying walls of a long-dead king's son fell
Time out of mind in the north, in the night,
And a ship stood wait for me under the isle and I came
With that treasure of word sometime spent
For my stay in this south.

THE YALE SERIES OF YOUNGER POETS, *which is designed to provide a publishing medium for the first volumes of promising poets, is open to men and women under forty who have not previously had a book of verse published. The Editor of the Series selects the winning volume in the annual contest and writes a preface for it. Manuscripts should be received before March 1 and should be addressed to the Editor, Yale Series of Younger Poets, Yale University Press, New Haven, Connecticut. Rules of the contest will be sent upon request.*

VOLUMES 48–50, 52–54 ARE IN PRINT.